How Do Tornadoes Form?

And Other Questions Kids Have About Weather

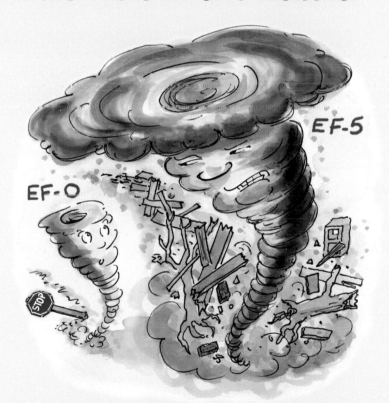

by Suzanne Slade   illustrated by Cary Pillo

PICTURE WINDOW BOOKS
a capstone imprint

Special thanks to our advisers for their expertise:

Nathan Harrington, Meteorologist
KEYC Television, North Mankato, Minnesota

Terry Flaherty, Ph.D., Professor of English
Minnesota State University, Mankato

Editor: Jill Kalz
Designer: Tracy Davies
Art Director: Nathan Gassman
Production Specialist: Jane Klenk
The illustrations in this book were created with ink and gouache.

Picture Window Books
1710 Roe Crest Drive
North Mankato, MN 56003
www.capstonepub.com

Library of Congress Cataloging-in-Publication Data
Slade, Suzanne.
How do tornadoes form? : and other questions kids have about
weather / by Suzanne Slade ; illustrated by Cary Pillo.
p. cm. — (Kids' questions)
Includes index.
ISBN 978-1-4048-6048-3 (library binding)
ISBN 978-1-4048-6731-4 (paperback)
1. Weather—Miscellanea—Juvenile literature. I. Pillo, Cary, ill.
II. Title.
QC981.3.S59 2010
551.6—dc22   2009038537

What makes the weather?

Margaux, age 7

Earth is covered in a blanket of gases called the atmosphere. Changes inside the atmosphere make weather. As the sun warms the land and water below the atmosphere, air moves. The sun's heat also turns water in lakes and oceans into water vapor. Heat, moving air, water vapor, and even the tilt of the planet affect Earth's weather.

Why does weather change?

Cassidy, age 7

Weather changes because of moving pockets of warm and cold air. These pockets are always moving around the planet, so our weather is always changing.

How does wind blow?
Robby, age 6

How fast can wind go?
Abhi, age 7

Earth gets its heat from the sun. Powerful rays heat up pockets of air near Earth's surface. The hot air rises. As the hot air goes up, colder air moves in to take its place. This air movement causes wind. The fastest surface wind ever recorded was 231 miles (370 kilometers) per hour. It was measured on Mount Washington. Winds inside a tornado, however, can move even faster!

What is the coldest place on Earth?

Hunter, age 9

The lowest temperature ever recorded on Earth was minus 128.6 degrees Fahrenheit (minus 89.2 degrees Celsius). It happened at Vostok, Antarctica, in July 1983.

What is the hottest temperature ever recorded?

Audrey, age 9

The highest temperature in the world was recorded in the town of El Azizia, in northern Africa. On September 13, 1922, it was a blazing 136 °F (58 °C)!

What is windchill?

second graders, Franklin Elementary

Windchill is how cold it feels on your skin when you mix temperature and wind. Let's say the temperature is 0 °F (minus 18 °C), and the wind is blowing at 20 miles (32 km) per hour. The windchill would be minus 22 °F (minus 30 °C). Wind makes the temperature feel colder.

What are clouds?
Annalisa, age 8

How many kinds of clouds are there?
Katie, age 6

CIRRUS

CIRROSTRATUS

CIRROCUMULUS

ALTOSTRATUS

ALTOCUMULUS

CUMULONIMBUS

STRATOCUMULUS

NIMBOSTRATUS

STRATUS

CUMULUS

Clouds are a collection of tiny drops of water and small ice crystals. There are 10 kinds of clouds. A cloud's name tells scientists how it was formed and its height.

How do clouds get their shapes?

Tim, age 6

Clouds are shaped by many things, including temperature, wind, and how much water is in the air. Cold temperatures usually make thin, wispy clouds. So does dry air. Fat, fluffy clouds often appear on warm, humid days.

How does rain start?

Zachary, age 6

When water warms up, it evaporates, or turns into gas. This gas, called water vapor, rises into the air. It then cools, turns back into water droplets, and forms clouds. This process is called condensation. The tiny droplets grow larger as more water vapor is gathered. In time, the droplets get so heavy they fall to the ground as precipitation. Rain and snow are kinds of precipitation.

What part of the world gets the least rain?

Annika, age 7

The Atacama Desert in Chile is the driest place in the world. It gets less than 0.004 inches (0.01 centimeters) of rain a year.

Atacama
UMBRELLAS

Why do rainbows form?

Hannah, age 8

Rainbows form when sunlight passes through falling raindrops. The drops of water sort the sunlight into seven different colors. The top color of a rainbow is always red, followed by orange, yellow, green, blue, dark blue (indigo), and purple (violet).

How can hail get so big?

second graders, Franklin Elementary School

A hailstone begins with a frozen raindrop. The droplet falls from the cold top of a cumulonimbus cloud to the warm bottom. There, water covers the icy droplet before wind carries it back up. The cold air freezes the water, making the hailstone bigger. Hail moves back and forth like this, gathering layers until it finally falls to the ground. The longer that hailstones stay in clouds, the bigger they become.

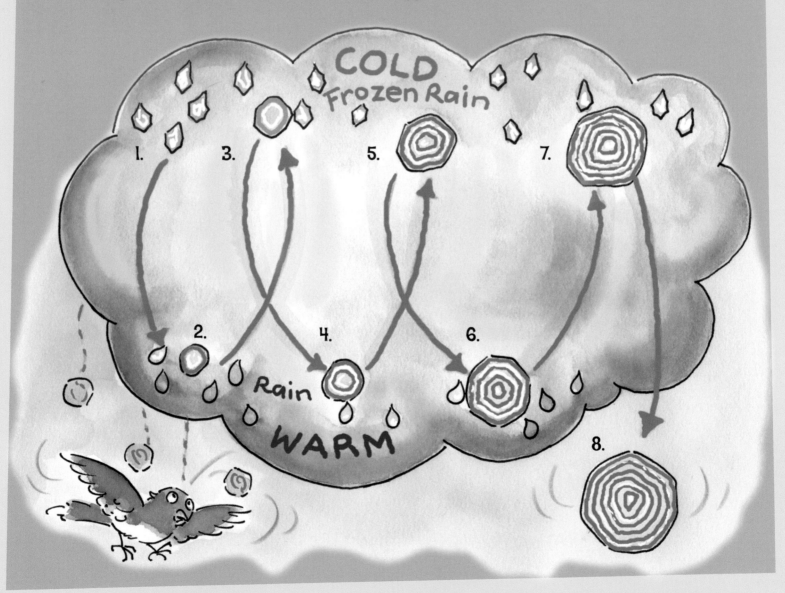

How many hailstones have fallen at once?

second graders, Franklin Elementary School

In 1950, a storm dropped 18 inches (46 cm) of hail on the small town of Selden, Kansas. It was impossible to count all the hailstones.

What is the largest hailstone on Earth?

Sydney, age 9

The biggest hailstone landed in Nebraska in 2003. Nearly the size of a soccer ball, the ice chunk measured 7 inches (17.8 cm) across. This huge hailstone is now kept in a Colorado lab.

How does snow get made?

Bryce, age 6

In winter, water droplets in clouds freeze and form ice crystals. The crystals stick together to form snowflakes. One snowflake may be made of hundreds of tiny crystals.

Does it snow in other places besides the United States?

Emily, age 7

Yes, snow falls in many other places around the world. Snow falls most often in places far from the equator or high in the mountains. Greenland, Antarctica, and the world's tallest mountaintops are covered with snow year-round.

14

Why is snow white instead of different colors?

Emily, age 6

An object's color is what color light bounces off it. When light hits snow, all colors bounce off. And when all colors mix together, they make white.

How does lightning form?
Beto, age 6

Winds inside storm clouds hurl ice crystals against one another. The crashing ice produces a negative charge in the cloud. When the negative charge in the cloud is attracted to a positive charge on the ground, lightning forms.

What will happen if you get struck by lightning?
Walker, age 7

When lightning strikes a person, he or she may black out, have his or her heart stop, or even die. To keep safe, stay inside a building during a storm. Stay there until 30 minutes after the last clap of thunder.

How does thunder boom?

Chad, age 5

Flashes of lightning make thunder. A bolt of lightning heats the air around it to 50,000 °F (27,782 °C). That's about five times hotter than the sun! This superheated air spreads out very fast, making a sound wave. The wave is the booming sound we hear as thunder.

How do tornadoes form?
Matt, age 7

Why do tornadoes look gray?
Perry, age 8

Tornadoes form inside cumulonimbus clouds. The tops of the clouds hold fast-moving cold air. The bottoms hold slow-moving warm air. When the cold air moves over the warm air, twisting funnels form. Funnels become tornadoes when they touch ground. Tornadoes get their dark color from the dirt they suck up.

Which part of the world gets the most twisters?

Anna, age 8

Three-fourths of all tornadoes happen in the southern United States. Texas gets more tornadoes than any other state.

Why do tornadoes knock down everything?

Alissa, age 6

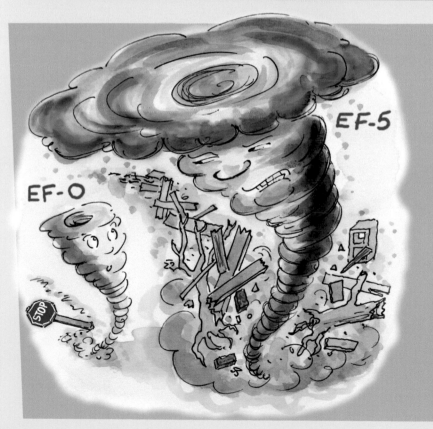

EF-5

EF-0

Scientists rate tornadoes with the Enhanced Fujita scale. EF-0 tornadoes are the weakest. They may lift up roof shingles. EF-5 tornadoes, the strongest, have winds of more than 200 miles (320 km) per hour. They knock down everything in their paths. Luckily, EF-5s are very rare. The United States has an average of just one per year.

How do hurricanes start?

Julia, age 5

Hurricanes start as small storms at sea. These storms gain strength from the heat rising from warm ocean waters. As Earth spins, the storms begin to swirl and move west. Winds can reach speeds of up to 180 miles (288 km) per hour. The center of a hurricane, however, is calm. It's called the eye.

How do you know when a hurricane is coming?

Kaitlyn, age 6

Meteorologists are always watching the weather. They try to figure out when a hurricane will come and where it will hit. TV and radio forecasters warn people in the hurricane's path. You usually can't see any signs of a hurricane from land until about 36 hours before it hits.

FIRST ALERT HURRICANE WATCH

ESTIMATED LANDFALL 10:00 PM

How do weather people know the weather before it happens?

Taylor, age 7

Forecasters on TV get their information from meteorologists. These scientists learn about changes in Earth's atmosphere by looking at satellite pictures. They also collect data from weather stations and weather balloons. Meteorologists use computers to show how the weather is expected to be.

SATELLITE

METEOROLOGIST

WEATHER 5

MONDAY COLD 20°

FORECASTER

TO LEARN MORE

More Books to Read

Eckart, Edana. *Watching the Weather.* New York: Children's Press, 2004.

Editors of Time for Kids. *Storms!* New York: HarperCollins, 2006.

Rabe, Tish. *Oh Say Can You Say What's the Weather Today? All About Weather.* New York: Random House, 2004.

Internet Sites

FactHound offers a safe, fun way to find Internet sites related to this book. All of the sites on FactHound have been researched by our staff.

Here's all you do:

Visit *www.facthound.com*

FactHound will fetch the best sites for you!

GLOSSARY

absorbed—taken in

atmosphere—a layer of gases surrounding a planet

equator—an imaginary line around the middle of Earth that separates it into two equal parts

humid—damp or moist

meteorologist—a scientist who studies weather

satellite—a machine that circles Earth in outer space and gathers information

surface wind—the wind measured at a standard distance from the ground

water vapor—the gas form of water

weather balloon—a large balloon that floats above Earth and gathers information about weather such as temperature and wind speed

weather station—equipment placed on land or at sea that gathers information about weather

INDEX

Look for all of the titles in the Kids' Questions series:

Did Dinosaurs Eat People?
And Other Questions Kids Have About Dinosaurs

Do All Bugs Have Wings?
And Other Questions Kids Have About Bugs

How Do Tornadoes Form?
And Other Questions Kids Have About Weather

What Is the Moon Made Of?
And Other Questions Kids Have About Space

What's Inside a Rattlesnake's Rattle?
And Other Questions Kids Have About Snakes

Who Invented Basketball?
And Other Questions Kids Have About Sports

Why Do Dogs Drool?
And Other Questions Kids Have About Dogs

Why Do My Teeth Fall Out?
And Other Questions Kids Have About the
Human Body